Morning Coffee

Morning Coffee

By

James R Simms

SIMMS BOOKS PUBLISHING

SIMMS BOOKS PUBLISHING

Publishers Since 2012

Published By Simms Books Publishing

Jonesboro, GA

Copyright © James R Simms, 2016

All rights reserved. No part of this book may be reproduced, scanned, or distributed in any print or electronic form without permission. Please do not participate in or encourage piracy of copyrighted materials in violation of the author's rights. Purchase only authorized editions.

Library of Congress Cataloging in Publication Data

James R Simms

MORNING COFFEE

ISBN: 978-0-9983311-1-9

Printed in the United States of America

Edited by Mary Hoekstra

Book Arrangement by Simms Books Publishing

Cover by Urias Brown, Michael Shield Studios

Dedicated to my children, family and friends. Live free, speak your mind, and love yourself unconditionally. Omar, your little brother is still working hard accomplishing my dreams, you taught me to speak my mind and live free without limitations. Mom, I'm learning everyday, I hear your wisdom still speaking to me and guiding me as I make a mark and build a legacy. Thank you! I love and miss you both. Rest Easy, I do this for you!

ALL I WANT TO DO IS WIN!!

Good Morning, Family! We have so many folks out here hurting, mentally, emotionally, physically and spiritually. They seem unable to get out of their own way. Where the mind goes, the body will follow. Let's put up a prayer for them right now and a prayer for you also. "God we look to you for freedom. Please free the mind of all those things that may hold us down: depression, sadness, jealousy, hate, and stagnation. We need to be free to do what we want when we want and be successful now! Not Tomorrow but now! When we get at least one victory, multiply it by 1000 and have our winning spirits rub off on the less fortunate so they can win also. Erase that Want to, and just Win! Amen!"

PEACE

Good Morning, Family! I hope this finds you in a space where your heart is light; your mind is at ease, your body is in a state of comfort, and love is all around you. All things are in your favor and things are going your way. If I have found you in turmoil, I pray for a release, a release of all that stresses you; sending good vibrations to build you up with hope and confidence. You have to know that everything is gonna be alright. Focus; meditate on it today and each day there after. I pray that you will find your peace. I love you.

GREATEST LOVE

The greatest possession a man can have is the love of a woman and children. You all are gifts. A man's job is to uplift both children and women, protect, provide, and make secure. That means if there's any discord, anger, sadness, insecurities, he is to fix those and remind that woman that they are working together to solve these issues. The only state a woman and children should ever reside in is Happiness! They are filled with it. They are content; nothing moves them to bitterness, because they are constantly reminded of how blessed they are, how they are encouraged to be themselves, and to strive for their best, not what the world around them thinks. There should be no fighting, because a man's job and mission is to bring peace to a woman; if there is no peace then you are not dealing with a mature situation. Look in the mirror or look at that man. Men are responsible and have work to do constantly, to improve himself, his life, and the lives of those around him. A man helps; he never puts anyone down, because when he points one finger, three are pointing back at him. His goal is to inspire, not tear down. Any action taken opposite of good renders that man a coward, not a man. Men can share, want to share, mentally, spiritually, and physically, to show his woman he cares. He helps her take down her walls and accepts her for who she is at that moment. He sees greatness in her that he wants her to see for herself. Two ways of thought cannot occupy the same

space; he can't be happy and she is upset; it won't work. Both will have to be of one accord. Woman has to surrender to a man who fits these attributes, but first she has to get herself together, mentally, so she will know who is right for her when she sees him. Woman! You attract who you are, be what you desire.

A KISS

Reassurance, the act that says 'I love you' without saying a word. The blessing bestowed upon the receiver, given out of love, protection, affection, an act of kindness unmatched. A kiss, a simple kiss will give you all of this and so much more. As you can see a kiss goes a long way! Have you had your kiss today?

MOTHER'S DAY

"THE PERFECT PURPOSE." Being a mother is one of the greatest gifts in the world and one with great responsibility. What you do and how you do it plays a big role in the lives of others. See it's not all about what you say; it's more about what you do, because eyes are watching. Little eyes, big eyes, and God's eyes. The role of mom and mother is not mistake free. You do and say some bad and wrong things in the process, but God knows your progress as you grow, because it's an experience that you grow and mature in while you are doing it and that's when wisdom takes over. Wisdom is passed down from your mom, your mom's mom and so on. A mother may not be perfect but her purpose is. Her job is to nurture and raise a child, protect and make sure that child's life is full of love, and teach them all the things that will help them become parents themselves one day. Mother: someone who is an extreme or ultimate example of her kind, especially in terms of scale. She is affectionate, caring, covering, a leader, a caretaker, the origin and producer and guide. The Example! Yes! THE PERFECT PURPOSE. This is for you being the woman who has been living out that purpose perfectly. Happy Mother's Day!

ARE YOU READY?

Good Morning, Family! I try to use my words to inspire others on a daily basis, as I experience life I try taking notes. It's understandable that no one gets it right all the time; we are human. It happens! Forging our way thru life, we please some and piss off others. What can you do? Just a part of life, ya know. But I can tell you this, as long as you live you will learn and being a student of life prepares you, at best, to be ready for any test.

KEEP FIGHTING

Good Morning, Family! I know it's hard and I can only imagine the struggle and pain that you're going thru. This is not the time to give up or give in! Just letting you know that I'm praying for you and I will offer any support that I can. So it is written, "When two or three are gathered in MY name I am with them." Don't worry because you and I make two and God is with you! Keeping you prayed up!

ONE MORE CHANCE

Good Morning, Family! There are situations in life when if you had a reset button at that very moment, you would press it. To either do it over again differently or actually not ever attempt to do it at all. For the times that you would want to go back and do it all again, but in a different way I believe the universe gives you the opportunity. It may be for love, friendship, clarity, or putting the pieces of the puzzle together to make sure it stays that way, together. Righting a wrong or completing a mission. Good news! While you still have life, you still have "One More Chance!"

NO NEED

Good Morning, Family! I have learned over the years that some things are meant to be left alone, not to be spoken of, addressed, or even shared. My next move, the who, what, where, when and how, and showing you what I have or don't have in my pockets. Everything has its time and place.

YOU'RE THE V.I.P

Good Morning, Family! Nowadays you see folks needing and wanting validation from others, so much so that they measure their own self-worth by it. I'll be damned if you or you think this way! You are more precious than silver and gold! God created you in such a way that your uniqueness is tailor-made. Yeah, you got it, and you're special! Tell them, "I'm not conceited but I do concede...I'm so freaking awesome!!! Honor your Creator by being awesome and let the others acknowledge your light!

FIND HAPPINESS

Good Morning, Family! I confess my faults. There! I'm done! You do the same and live life guilt free. Yeah, we all have issues at some point in life, so there's no need to relive them. Its old news; learn from them and move on. Now, it's all about growth and happiness! Go get you some! Happiness is at the door saying, "Hey I missed you! Where have you been?" Get your mind right.

DEAR MAMA

I miss hugs and kisses from you, how you would comb my hair, put Vaseline on my face, speak to me, and kiss me on my forehead when I was sick. I could always depend on you to make sense of things; you had that wisdom that made me think before I reacted. You were selfless and always helping others. You never gave a thought about it; you just gave and shared yourself with others, even when it took away from your personal time with us. You were showing us something. You had the best sense of humor and could make anyone smile, even when you yourself were having a bad day. You stressed the importance of priorities and living within your means, raising your quality of life and making sure that "you pay yourself first" was something we should never forget. Never give too much of yourself, save something for yourself. It's all about balance. Self-love and respect and call it like it is, if it don't mix it just won't work. Your heart loved and your bad side was where we never wanted to be. Your undying faith in God and belief "that if it didn't please God it would not be, good or bad." I can still hear you say, "This Too Shall Pass," encouraging me to look past the mountain in front of me and call out, "Mountain Move!" You would always remind me of these things when I was going thru a rough spot in my life. "Where's God in your life," you would ask me, knowing that if I took it to HIM then everything would all work out. Mom, I'm still having a problem...HE didn't heal you and took you away from me. I miss you, Mom!

SPREAD LOVE

Good Morning, Family! Man, I can tell you, for a lot of us, it has been a rough couple of years. It's been real rough and it seems like it hasn't stopped yet. Sometimes, it's human nature for us to forget; at times we are real passionate about something, all up in arms, then that fire dies out and we go on with our normal lives. Never forget! If it wasn't for the rain...Yall don't hear me! Be thankful for everything given and lost. Tell someone, "I love you." Share that love with your family, friends, and strangers. Just know that someone will appreciate it more than you know. I Love You!

IF HEAVEN HAD VISITING HOURS

If Heaven had visiting hours...I would spend all of my time with you, forget about this life here and be with you. This hole in my heart...no one can fill right now. The sorrow grabs a hold of me at different times of the day and all I do is stop whatever I'm doing and cry. There is no being tough; sucking this up, man'n up cause I miss you.

WHEN ALL ELSE FAILS...HERE COMES GOD

Good Morning, Family! You have lost touch; things are not going your way; the mountains that you climbed before seem just a little bit higher today. But have faith, determination, and stay true to yourself, your mission and your art. Believe that one day it will touch someone's heart, so they go to bat for you and see what you see. Greater is HE that is in me! Give thanks for everything; your dreams can get their wings and you will fly high! It can all happen in a twinkling of an eye. God is good All the Time!

TIME WAITS FOR NO MAN

Time waits for no one! Make the best of your time while you are here! Use it wisely and lending your attention to those things that are worth your time. For today, "Continuing Education" is time well spent. Knowledge is Power!

NO DAYS OFF

Good Morning, Family! I spoke to a CEO yesterday morning and what he said stuck with me. He said, "Even though I had to go to work on my day off, it was ok...not what I wanted to do but what I had to do. My job is part of my calling, to touch people, influence them in a positive way." Message! So whenever you find the job that God has called you to...it is a blessing to go to work. Live out your calling and enjoy it!

THREE TYPES OF FEMALES

I wish I was told this priceless piece of information earlier in life, but I guess it's all in the timing. "There are three types of females." You have; a woman, a bitch, and a whore. Not all females are women and not all bitches are whores. Yelp, I said it. Unfortunately this classification holds true. Young female which one are you? Young male, you have to use this guide in order to avoid two out of the three. A woman is respectful, kind hearted, responsible and looks after herself, her children, and others. A bitch makes excuses of why she can't do anything; she hates to see anyone do better than she, and she is a hater, difficult to deal with, and never satisfied. She is unrealistic and normally puts a male, her hobbies, going out, and her time before her children. A whore has no real moral compass; she lets her lower desires guide her and thinks her body will pay her way. She dresses, acts, and conducts her life like a woman of the night. It's a "fuck you pay me mentality." Everyone owes her and she sexualizes everything. She wears her uniform proudly, scantily clad. Truth is some females may exhibit a little of each ones qualities, but don't settle for less. Men choose wisely!

THREE TYPES OF MALES

Now let's elevate the conversation, my brother! Let's look at the three classifications of a male in the world; Niggas, Bitch Ass Niggas and Men (skin color not included)

1. Niggas: ignorant, sub-human, inferior, heartless, irresponsible, and disloyal (in a hood since: Thugs and Go Hard, fake me out gangsters) manipulators, thieves, cheaters and control freaks.

2. Bitch Ass Niggas: same as Niggas, always has an excuse, will stab you in the back whenever you give them a chance, not equipped to handle any responsibility, a con man, and reverts to name calling because he has no leg to stand on.

3. Men or a Man; intelligent, responsible, confident, does not beg or borrow, powerful and knows how to manage his power of influence and respect correctly, secure in himself, always in the pursuit of greatness. In mind body and spirit, speaks life, love and encouragement; never a playa hater, he does not play games. He understands his relationship with God and works every day to put it into practice. He takes care of his kids and makes no excuses. A protector and puts the duty of caring for others before anything else. He gives a firm handshake and looks you dead in the eyes.

WHATS IN A NAME

Good Morning, Family! What's in a name? Be very careful of what you call yourself! Shakespeare questioned, "What's in a name?" What do you call yourself? As a man thinketh so is he! Think better thoughts and strive to be and do better in this life. Stop with the words of discouragement; give hope and life thru the words that you speak! Parents Stop it! Yes you! Stop calling your child dumb, trifling, and every other damn word that you use when speaking to them that is not helping them. This simple word that I hear a lot and its not cute at all; "Bad," or such and such they bad, she just bad, he just bad. No you just ignorant! Stop it! Because they will be whatever you call them and answer to it and live it! Family! Remember this also "It's not what they call you it's what you answer to."

COLOR BLIND

It's amazing how kids are color blind. My kids make friends everywhere they go, sitting down eating ice cream turns into an international game of tag! To be a kid again! One of the parents wanted to up and leave but seeing how much fun the kids were having, they stayed. We sparked up a conversation, which probably would not happen on a regular day when strangers pass by and mind their business. I guess its human nature to be somewhat closed off to people you don't know…my correction, adult nature. As we get older, we draw lines in the sand, stick to what we are comfortable with, live out the life we were taught to have, and how to be and conduct ourselves. Kids on the other hand haven't gotten to that part just yet; they just wanna have fun and it doesn't matter where that other child came from, skin color or background. The children brought us together and you know we should let down our guards more often. We all were in the same boat, 'guarded' against the unknown. To be a kid again.

NOT MY PRESIDENT

Good Morning Family! Who did you vote for? I thought I voted for The Commander and Chief and Leader of the Free World. Damn! What happened? I thought the popular vote counted, not true at all, yeah learned that more than 12 years ago. Not again, is what came to mind, but this right here is crazy! Yeah way different this time. This man boasted about really not giving a fuck! Mexicans, Muslims, and anyone who disagreed with him and his policies will face his rath! No one took him too serious just sat back and laughed. "No he can't do that!" "They won't let him do it!" Funny thing is... they just did! Electing him President! "WE THE PEOPLE" I don't think they were talking about us, the voters, but who ever runs the Electoral College, yeah they got that! Students of history I ask you to share your thoughts, I know history will surely repeat itself if we don't look at it for what is can and will become. Reminds me of Hitler when the same kind of people yelled "It can't be done!" "He just can go around and just kill or get rid of people because of their nationality and culture!" We are faced with a heavy burden and a lot of folks' lives are at stake, I'm sure you know that the expulsion of millions of people from this land will be sure nuff war, when they go to the school houses and knocking on doors. No I didn't see this coming and it wasn't in a dream, I read it before in history books and I'm betting on a different outcome. People have become more tolerant and free thinkers and then some! We will be fighting for our lives and the lives of all those people we love and learned to love. One Love! God is my President!

RELEASE RELIGION'S BAGGAGE

What you believe and what you think are indicative of your moral and religious compass. Doctrine that's created by man will have you serving the wrong things. As a man thinketh so is he. Take man out of the equation and what he taught you to believe, and go by logic. You believe in a heaven man told you about yet no one dead has ever come back to tell you what heaven is like. We believe in a mystery we will live in fantasy while the ones who know the truth steal the chance we have at a heaven on earth. Heaven and Hell are conditions...Heaven is what you make it and Hell is what you go thru. Man sells us fairytales to keep our third eyes blind and our minds busy with nonsense. For example, when have you ever heard a bunny rabbit talk? Or lay eggs? Simple things keep a man's mind simple when he grows up. Santa Claus has nothing to do with Jesus; "bait and switch" has your mind thinking about other things, but not about the truth. Jesus was killed, not Him laying His life down for all our sins. He brought salvation to the wicked of the world to cleanse their hearts and souls to do right. He laid down His life in doing so. His teachings of love and turning away from evil fell on deaf ears; the very people He came to save killed Him. He was here for the ones who were not following rules that were sent down from God Himself. Who did He hang out with? The poor, the prostitutes, the sick. Who did He warn? The rich, evil rulers, they murdered Him then romanticize His death

as a tribute to saving everyone's souls. The evil that men do. Our beloved preachers, who declare they are "Christ Like," are not even close to Him. They profess with their mouths but check their technique the bad apples will spoil the bunch. Religion? No thank you. I am releasing the rope that binds it back together freeing me of the hypocrisy.

YOU'RE ALWAYS ON MY MIND

Good Morning, Family! You're always on my mind. I know that life is a very fragile existence and we can be here today, gone tomorrow, so I plan to send verbal roses to you every day from this point on. I see that there is always a need for a few things in life: prayer, patience, understanding and love. One cannot fully recover, find peace, and thrive without them. So this is my gift to you, so you will know that no matter what, if it all falls down, there is still another person out here holding you up in prayer and love, no matter what.

I WAS JUST LIKE YOU

Wake up in the morning ready to hate something, mad because I don't have nothing, nothing better to do than hurt the next man, the power that I feel is burning inside of me, ready to release when I have that gun in hand. Man! You can't tell me shit! Scheming and planning on the next person that step up and just where my bullets will hit. Yeah, I wish a nigga would! I live for my block, die for my block, I represent my hood! This hate is deeply rooted; I can't hear any of the wisdom the elders are kicking because I stay high, fucked up, tweaking...man I'm zooted! Smoked out, brain fried, lungs all polluted!

Hell, burn 'em up! I'm going out like Bob Marley! Yeah, ball out till I fall out! I roll like my favorite Italian mafia movie, "Scarface!"

Fast-forward ten years and here I am...no longer like you. I have found better things to do with my time; I love myself and want to live. No longer do I harbor the hate that I held for those who look just-like-me. I stopped the cycle of violence, and most of all, ignorance. Being smart, educated and doing something worth living for is my new thirst and I give more when I didn't give a damn to begin with. Looking back, I felt so ashamed of what I was. When was it ever fashionable to be dumb and destructive?

Well, it used to be. Not anymore. Wow, I can't believe that for years we reduced a great man like Bob Marley to a splif

or a joint of weed, 420. FYI, Bob Marley did not die from smoking weed, it was a toe infection that spread throughout his body...or even worse his consciousness in his songs started reaching so many people, changing the way they thought of the world that Someone took him out. My way of thinking was all messed up, now I can see that the Italian tough guy that I wanted to be, from my favorite movie, was not Frank. It was Tony!

News Flash! Tony was Cuban! Wow, ignorance is bliss. I bet, if you asked, the narrative would be the same. "My favorite Italian gangsta movie is 'Scarface.' JUST SOUND SO STUPID. I can't believe I thought the same way... We have to do better.

NOT RELIGIOUS

I only seek truth in this life and truth will set you free. I have taken a step back years ago to look at every religion. I have to correct you; I am not Rastafarian, Christian, Muslim, Jewish or Catholic. They do not hold the patent on Life I agree with a lot of what they teach, but again, a man coined the name to a way of life and doctrine. We can get along, but man cannot follow two leaders. My understanding is universal; I don't get caught up in organized religion… just another form of slavery and control. I don't need a middleman when it comes to me speaking to God. No thank you. I'm good. But as far as how I see things and having lived a life with plenty of experiences, I have come to this conclusion and train of thought: so I took the truths and expelled any falsehoods of man out of my thought process and I am "Spiritual." I believe in God, but not the BS that most religious doctrines try to feed you. Charity goes to the needy, not the minister or preacher, or to a building fund, or even to God in monetary means. He judges you on what you do and give in the process of doing good, not by people not giving to someone who professes the word but don't live it themselves, then come up with the excuse, "I'm human." Naw, dude, you representing God, then all ya'll better be like the Pope but he prolly got skeletons too. Who knows, just not for the world to see lol. But I'm good.

MY SOURCE

Good Morning, Family! The Most High God is my strength and source of power! I am human and sometimes I forget that when I am going thru hell all I have to do is call on HIM. The Great I AM! We have to stay consistent! But yall don't hear me tho! Yes stay consistent in the WORD and seek HIM not just on Sundays or days that are not going your way, but EVERYDAY! From the time you wake up till the time that you go to sleep you have to stay in communication with God. We find ourselves really only calling out to HIM when we need some help. Make it routine that you call on HIM all thru the day, thanking him at every step so that HE will do as he promised and 'go ahead of you and clear the way.'

WAVE OF LOVE

Sounds of water clashing and wind claps from the wings of nearby birds, sitting there I can feel the warmth from the ascending sun as it makes its way into the sea. The beautiful colors adorn your skin, crimson, yellows, blues turned to brilliant purples, and you smile as I touch your hand. We walk, forging thru white sand paradise, in tune with this kaleidoscope of hues and sun beaten sky. Above us a southern wind blows, taking with it a rich scent of your perfume as it intoxicates my nose, giving me a euphoric spike that sends my senses into a love tumble, reaching out, bringing you closer, I steal a kiss. We sit and enjoy the remainder of the day... Beachside love.

IF I SHOULD DIE

Good Morning, Family! Just remember if I die, let them know I was only protecting myself; my children have orders to grow up and avenge me, to burn this shit down! Grow up and unite people against this bullshit. Self-preservation is first priority, so If I am killed, you know I did nothing wrong. Born black, loving my neighbor. I didn't do it! If I survive, having to kill someone to save our lives. Come to my defense! Whatever the fuck the news wants to show, or whatever lies they fabricate, just know I didn't do it. It's sad that it has to be this way...I do not live in fear. I'm fully aware of what's going on in this world and the odds of me dying by the hands of a black man or a racist cop are about even. Yeah, sad to say, but that is reality nowadays and it makes no damn sense. So when you wonder why I'm on edge all the time, it's because this ain't living...the way they do my life. But the odds I can change are reaching out to my brother and appealing to his common sense. We need to come together, the cops I won't waste my breath, just pray God has my back and those around me. I spoke to my brothers this morning, my gang brothers, I reached out to some high-ranking members and we have come to an agreement on this front; the time is now... stopping the violence. You know we still have some loose ends out there in the ranks, copycat wannabes and those who thrive and live off of killing their own kind. That's a problem, but we will soon fix that issue. Yeah, the killings may not stop immediately but we gonna walk those

individuals down and deal with them, because we have bigger fish to fry. If I should die, I was on the job! I was being part of the solution and not the problem. It's time to clean house. Now don't get me wrong, the devil will always fuel the fire to keep this shit going, but believe me, it will stop one way or another. So it has come to this and now the conversation has started. Don't get frustrated, Rome wasn't built in a day...right? Protect your essence! Some of you will never understand how it is to live in this skin! I'm doing my part to solve this problem. What about you?

TRUE SACRIFICE

Good Morning, Family! Well take a deep breath. Life is so fragile. Peace to all those souls who have crossed over, heads hang low in prayer, as we look toward the future, praying for the best. Now is the time to take advantage of the time we have and fill it with happiness and make it count; here to making it count! We may have to make big sacrifices to enable this happiness, but in the end it will be necessary and worth it...live for the now.

A MOTHER'S LOVE

I know that a mother is a woman who has children that she cares for and works hard to raise them and protects them. She does the best she can; sometimes getting it wrong but ultimately, she gets it right. There's no handbook, she learns, as she grows, the proof is in the pudding, her role as a parent changes as the little ones grow. Never a dull moment because that's how it's supposed to be; she takes the bumps and bruises and hard knocks on this long journey. Being a mother is not an easy task by far. Mother, Mom...without her...none of us would be here. She combs your hair, zippins your jacket to keep you warm, applying vaseline on your face to keep it from drying, helping you get dressed and showing you how to tie your shoe laces, the small things that matter the most when I look back and what I miss the most...

YOU AINT SHIT!

Ok...this one's for you. So you claim, Africans, Muslims, Christians, Hebrews who claim they about the cause, I ain't seen none of you kill for our slain youth...pause...That's the Gotdamn Truth. Wanna dispute it then say my name six times, in your feelings? The sun still shines...or should I say son, shid cause ya'll get caught up in metaphors, word play; knowledge ain't shit if you don't use it! Yeah, that's cute, you know your history, but a fool with knowledge can't do shit for me and it shows...how many more times we gonna see us killing us and they killing us and put that to an end? Ohh ohh when the revolution begins! Manye fuck that you cowardice sheep! It's been here that last fucking ten years. And from YOU?! I ain't even hear a peep. Yeah, it's a novel idea to post shit, talking about what you gonna do...the revolution is here...please let me know again what you gon do? A youngin was killed the other day in cold blood and the system freed his killer and I ain't seen you take him out. Shut your fucking mouth! Yeah ya'll talking loud and ain't gonna do shit! Hopefully this hits home...yeah right where you sit. You gots nothing for me and you ain't gonna do shit! Pro-black? Yeah, you a waste of fucking space...how does that feel to taste the blood in your mouth having a nerve to fix your damn lips and disrespect your elders out here cow towing faking all the while tryna figure out, looking the part ain't playing the part you stupid motherfuckers, lose one take one make 'em all suffer! Nah, too much for you cause you want to stay

confined behind your computers in your nice home, talking reckless like you really go like that. Sorry I object to that! Strong! So keep singing that same song...We shall overcome one day....the time is now but I can't seem to find any soldiers, just lost minds, a modern day slave on Social media, doing it for the yeah it rhymes with wine... And utttutuhh! Don't even say shit! Fuck you and them pussy ass niggas you ride wit! Like I said... checkmate you should be more humble but you play with strangers choosing wrong words that can seal your fate. Be quick to entertain strangers and beware of how you treat them because you may be in the presence of Angels... I see wisdom is not one of your strong suits, still a baby in this game tighten up... I can tell you a tale but you already know that there are two, which one did you choose? The devils and the Real Gods will have their way separating those who professes with their tongue but their hearts are nowhere to be found. Stop frontin cause you ain't about that life you fucking clown!

MY BIRTHDAY

Hello...it's me...Tomorrow is my birthday, a day I should feel excited about but I am terrified and sad about tomorrow. I have heard, over and over again, and sometimes I tell myself, "Don't worry, pray; if you gonna pray don't worry and if you worry...why pray?" Different milestones in life are times where you are either happy or have some worry. This is a great milestone in my life because I never thought that I would make it here, and now making it here I never thought I would not have my mom and brother here to give me that call to wish me Happy Birthday. My mom would remind me and give me a call on the 9th and tell me at 12:01 am morning of March 10th, was my official introduction to this world and she had all the hopes and dreams riding on a healthy baby boy. I struggle with the thought of what's around the corner, and it really fucks with me; all the wrong I've done in life and the things I've done in life that was just who I am, my reaction, my intentions and my thoughts. I struggle with my time and it running out. I can't be all things to everyone; I can only be me but I'm torn because my life is of service to God and for others. I am a people pleaser and I'm a good dude. I am turning that corner now, facing the next big step in my life, a procedure the day after my birthday and another shortly following. Just to be sure. I am hopeful and staying in prayer, but I am shaking in my boots for sure. There has not been a lot in life that has had me shook like this. I do have something to say, so you

know it's weighing heavy on my mind. I cried today and more than likely I will cry tomorrow. I'm a strong dude, I keep telling myself, but I can see 15 and 11 year old me when I look into my babies' eyes. I cannot let them down and I can't let the many that truly love me down. If you felt I've been distant, it's not personal, and I deal with mine in silence; that's the only way I know how. I know it has to be a good year, cause with all the fucked up shit going on, there's only one way and that's up. Don't be alarmed; just me wearing my heart on my sleeve, and yeah, it got me, caught me, lol slipping but I'm back up. Thank you all, yeah, I haven't been myself but I pray I can get back to it soon. Hey, I'ma smile thru it and damn sure give it my best.

TRUST THE PROCESS

Focus... People who leave your life, who don't make the cut, all served a purpose. When there is change going on in your life, God is at work. HE will put it on the hearts and minds of those who encounter you to be in your favor. You are a great example of a good person and you have an energy that draws people to you. Continue to stay grounded and humble. Go to bed tonight, counting your blessings, and wake up doing the same.

THE DEVIL WILL NOT WIN

Good Morning, Family! I pray that you are in good spirits and in good health. I will send up multiple prayers for you. Understand the time in which we live in; the devil is working overtime to try and take us out! I wish that I can just say that it's about just skin color alone. We are also facing an even larger problem and that has to do with classism; how much money you have and the influence that you hold. This system is out to destroy the little man, black, brown, yellow and white. Think its rhetoric if you want to and see how the policies change right before your eyes. We all have to be smart about this to stop the devil's plan. Look at the world today and those are the tell-tale signs that the devil is in full control and is about to do something big. You know the best lie he ever told was to convince the world that he did not exist. Now you know people can do mean and treacherous things, but think there can't actually be a devil, well think again. Stealing away your hopes and dreams, your hard earned money from a job that you busted your ass off day in and day out only to see very little revenue or none at all. Losing the very job that helped put food on your table, but now you have lost it by someone manipulating the system and creating an uneven playing field. He is real! Look at what's going on today! Family if you don't know, now you know! We are seeing the devil's work in action. We all need to get together on this and create a united front, they may kill some, but God has our back! He Helps Those Whom Help Themselves.

THIS TOO SHALL PASS

Good Morning, Family! "THIS TOO SHALL PASS." One of many sayings that my mother would tell me, is that no matter what the circumstance and situation, it will get better. I say better in a sense that you can deal with it and be sane again. We have all lost a loved one, some of us most recently, and the pain will never go away. I encourage you to try to look at the bright side of things and cherish the memories you had with them, good or bad. Make your life a shining example by being happy, sharing love like they would have wanted us to be. I know you're going thru it right now. I am here with you. Just know that God will send you a comforter to ease your pain and help you refocus on the love. I'm human also; I have so many regrets... Turn those into achievements, because they are watching us and wouldn't that be great! Your success and happiness dedicated to them. Remember, "THIS TOO SHALL PASS." I love you. Have a memorable weekend!

WHEN I FELL IN LOVE

The very first time we spoke and you shared your story and life, I knew you were a special woman. I was drawn to you. Then, when we were able to meet face to face, something else happened; I saw beauty in the heavens, God's Majesty, mother of civilization, Queen of the Universe! You! Nubian Queen! A face of a Goddess and body of an Angel, well crafted by the Best Artists in this solar system! A vision of pure perfection. I thought to myself once laying eyes on you, "Damn she is Sooo bad." I could not find a single flaw! Everything fit perfectly, and if I hadn't even had a conversation with you before I would still feel the same way, on sight. My mind wondered and asked over and over again, whoever is letting this woman down and go, is surely a damn fool and truly has to be blind, deaf and dumb. Your presence spoke even more volumes your poise and demeanor was so relaxing. Captivated by your spirit, I instantly fell for you. That moment in life was both refreshing and believable, that there were still great women out here and it was evident that I was sitting across from one! Yes, you made me a believer in the perfection of a woman, because even your dirt is part of it all. Yes you may feel that it's not, but you have met a person who loves the crust of you and proclaims that it's still all good. We all have gone astray plenty of times in our lives but it will never diminish our worth, and you are worth more than worth it. I know your struggle and who you are, because there is someone looking who thinks of all your

failures as successes, pitfalls as learning experiences, and bad decisions as great ones, cause in the end, this is what has made you who you are now. Someone looks at you in awe, seeing your crown is still intact and your light still shines brighter than any others. Your beauty is unmatched.

BEAUTIFUL WOMAN ISSUES

You are welcome. I call it "beautiful woman issues." It seems that the most beautiful ones go thru the most trying times. I know it has to do, alot of times, with what has happened to you in the past; subconsciously you go after certain men in life that do nothing for you mentally and spiritually. Love and physical contact for women is spiritual and emotional. For men it's visual and physical, for those men who have no ability to think outside the box and know how a woman works. Touching a woman physically does two things: it awakens her emotions and taps on her spiritual shoulder. It gets her attention, but keeping her attention has alot more work involved. A full connection has to be where all of the elements match and that woman know and feels full. There is no back and forth; she feels so good about herself and self worth; she smiles on the inside and longs to have that man with her. It brings total joy and pleasure; she is at peace. But only when she finds the connection and lets her emotions and logic guide her. Does she want someone that makes her feel good or someone who makes sure she is good? Love should never be something you have to work on, it just is and both parties can only give what they have. If there's no love there, it feels like a job or debt or pain. Love is simple and giving. Have you ever been touched with words? Touched in a way that it stays with you, and each time it's better than the last time? If it ain't Spiritual, Emotional, Comforting, Logical and Easy...it's not love.

PRETTY WOMEN

Now I done been around the world and seen and met plenty of "pretty women" but it's something about you, maybe it's what's in your eyes that tell your story, something in your voice or just your presence that just speaks to me. Honestly and truly, I find no faults about you that would keep me from being deeply in love with you. So just know that's what you are dealing with, a masterpiece. Go look in the mirror and see it for yourself! God has crafted such a beautiful woman staring back at you. Forget about what man has said. Hell, those fools are blind anyway! You are the epitome of what a Goddess is! Mannn! Let me tell you! Perfect! Your skin, your eyes, your face, lips, neckline, cheeks, beauty moles, teeth, your body… the envy of the world cause everybody wanna be like you, look like you. They get plastic surgery, tans, body augmentation, the whole nine, just trying to capture some similarities of you! You are the Prototype! Please take the time to look at yourself and soak it all in; you are the most beautiful woman in the world. Remember the Hate always go up, up to the one who naturally wears the crown. Fix your crown, Baby! I'm more than a fan. I bow to your greatness! So if you're not being treated as the Queen you are, then get back on your throne, cause you deserve better and the best anyone can give to you, their heart, loyalty and admiration that should be bestowed on you everyday. To a woman's heart is her mind.

REAP WHAT YOU SOW

Good Morning, Family! I have grown to love the life that I live right now, the life I live today. "What you do in the dark will soon come to light." I never really understood those words until the things that I hid from others, the moves that I made without anyone knowing, came back and bit me. What we do in this world, which may have harmed or wronged another person, comes back to us in some way, fashion and form. I thought that I could get away with it. I knew that it was a time limit to it; stealing, scheming, lying and even a little bodily harm was my M.O. But you would have never questioned it because I had so much Charm. A good guy; yeah, you never heard shit about me; real bad boys move in silence. I don't need any fanfare or notoriety. Yeah, that's where a lot of you go wrong; all on Front Street letting everyone know your biz. I figured I could have a nice run, do my dirty in silence and it will never catch up to me, just as long as no one truly knew what I was doing. Well, just a couple of my friends and me. My road dogs, we tore shit up and you could never really tell who was the culprit we hid it so well. Shit got deep and it caught up to us that one fateful day, no more robbing, killing, well...I never stayed around to see, if they made it or not, it was either them or me and I'm still here breathing. It was all a setup from the get go. We were like 13 deep strapped with high powered joints, toolies, and handguns. Shit! It's a hit! Damn we never saw it coming! 5 of them got the drop on us with AK's spit'n and dumping.

Everybody is hit. I caught two in the leg, my man in front of me; his body was ravaged with bullets. I caught a thru-n-thru which hit me in the forehead. I grabbed my tool and started shooting until my 100 round clip was empty. At one moment I closed my eyes, accepting death in the hail of bullet fire. I was hit two more times, then silence. No more loud barrage of automatic guns rumbling thru the air, now deep cries and sounds of the ocean eclipsed the deafening tone. Death was upon us all around, blood seeping out of torn flesh. I could hear my associates and good friends take their last breaths and our enemies call out for help. I stood up and looked around; there was no one left. 12 of my men slowly dying and most of them dead. And my enemies? I had to finish one of them off with three shots to the head. We had reaped what we sowed, we stole from those who were dealing in death, to us a great cause, but it was still theft. Either way you look at it, we were in the wrong. I survived! I promised myself from that day forth to go straight. Hell I was given one more chance, which none of the other 17 had the luxury, damn hell is hot and karma is a bitch.

DON'T KNOW WHO THEY DEALING WITH

Good Morning, Family! I know there will be harder times ahead, just wait and see. Now is not the time to get tired, because we have great work to do. Brother! Know thyself! If you don't know now you know! You are greater than you know. I am with you! In the trenches, navigating through this life, looking off into the future may seem bleak, for those who do not know. Know this...You will survive. We have been here before and still we rise. Have no fear of man and of all of his weaponry; it won't save him as he battles with God. Keep your mind busy with good things that will help others and be your brothers' keeper. It is said that "Man Plans a Plan and God plans a Plan and surely God is the best of Planners." So fear not, go by God's Plan and rebuke the devil. Seek the heart of God, the fearlessness and steady rock and lean on that understanding that "No weapon formed against you shall prosper!" My Sister! Guard yourselves against the wickedness that the devil has created for you and your children. Be aware of the poisons that they have manufactured to infect you and stunt your seeds natural growth. We are all God's children and they will not win against us!

GO PLAY IN TRAFFIC

Good Morning, Family! We don't have time for the bullshit! You know; the lying ass, young minded, super ignorant, uneducated, with no common sense brainless fucks out here who want to try you. Unfortunately, we have a lot of them running around nowadays and by some mix-up in the damn matrix they are winning! Do your best to stay away from them so that you do not catch a charge. It's too many of them out here and I don't have enough bail money for all of you, so count to ten and keep it moving!

COMFORTABLE IN YOUR SKIN

No problem. It's easy to speak that of you because it's the truth. Everyone needs a word of encouragement and acknowledgement; actions may speak louder than words, only when the correct words are not consistently spoken. We are human and are allowed to fail a few times, but once we know better, we do better; no more excuses, "When I was a child I thought as a child but when I became mature (grown, adult) I put away childish things." That goes for every aspect in your life; do away with childish things and thoughts. That man could not possibly be good for you if you argue like little children over a misunderstanding or immature feelings. Being a Grown man or woman is to be secure and Security is God-Body, in essence and attributes. So a male who is secure and patient is a man, little boys no matter the height, weight or age, still do exist. A man is responsible for his happiness, and the happiness of others around him, to comfort and protect. Ask yourself, have you known those feelings? If not, you have not found your helpmate. Vice versa for women. Be secure and allow yourself to define you and keep you. Value your essence; know thyself first.

BOSS UP

Good Morning, Family! There comes a time in our lives when we are put to the test, challenged, a heavy burden is laid on our shoulders. Step up to the challenge, pass that test, and shoulder the weight! Your help may not come from others; they will leave you with the decision on your own, to sink or swim. Prove it to yourself that you are more than able; do not shrink from your responsibilities! Step up and get it done!

FATHERS

Good Morning, Family! Too many of us know what deadbeats are, scumbags, baby daddies, no good men, liars, procrastinators, pure trash. Very few, and this is unfortunate indeed, will ever acknowledge a real Father, Daddy, however you may call him. I salute all the Fathers who have not abandoned their jobs in the face of adversity when that woman chose to work against you and not with you. Yes you heard me right! There are some women who would rather work against a real man than see him doing right by his children, because they did not work out. I say to you men, stay strong and keep doing what you need to do in your children's lives. I believe that there is nothing in this world that can stop you from your job! Father, a man who takes care of his responsibility his child or children, and makes no excuses, he just does it. He believes that his presence is needed and he does what needs to be done for his child/children, his presence, phone calls, notes, taking them out, spending time, and not always money. Without question, it has everything to do with life's lessons and wisdom that can be shared and handed down from a man to his seed. Don't let the bullshit get in the way with arguing and making it about greed. That's a whole other story! Fathers, remember what you do will affect more than just you, your sin can be revisited on your children, so mind yourself with great control and constrain. We know that we all are not saints. But keep at it and know that you are here for a greater cause and reason beyond your needs; your job is to care for and nurture your seeds. Happy Father's Day!

THE ONE THAT GOT AWAY

I am out here chasing what might have been. Haven't found your clone, because in the end, there is only one you. I guess I have to settle for what it's not, and search for a look alike and listen and wait for a heart like yours, a vibe like yours, that's undeniable. But this puts me in an awkward place, which I've never experienced before. I've been conditioned to have what I wanted and praised my woman, who is next to God, with all of my love and affection, warming her heart and comforting her mind with my all, words, care and actions, because I am the Truth. I love to infinity, but this right here has broken me… made me feel like a failure, peering from a window, seeking that solidarity with you, but there is none. We won't share that intimate moonlit night, being woken up by the sun's rays on lazy Saturday mornings, me and you all into one. It's a fantasy; I swore it would come true. I know your inner beauty is neck and neck with your outer beauty, and he swears he loves you. Wishful thinking on my part, I guess. But you, my dear, are truly what dreams are made of…black woman magic. I'm not sorry I feel this way about you…

FEAR OF LOVE

You are! But fear is what keeps all of us away from things. That is our prison. I remember I used to feel guilty as hell, wanting to be happy and free, wondering what the hell my ex was doing and with whom, lol. And after a while, I didn't want to love anyone else, because I thought it would turn out the same way. That's a prison; JHUD said "...this love is a prison now I'm busting out!" You have to ask yourself and put it into perspective the whys and hows? I couldn't enjoy being with another woman because I was used to being with her and she being with me. Just used to it. The question is; "Just what feeds your soul?" Will your mistakes or your imperfections be issues or jewels? Loving the crust of someone, or is it perception? Knowing the why shows you really love that person even more. Example: A man had a problem cheating in his past relationship; you know he craved something that woman could not give him. The woman, who knows and recognizes that issue, loves him for his flaws; she will have that conversation that most women don't and get to the heart of his cheating. She will give him what he desires, both physically and emotionally... not just one, cause a man who cheats needs both to keep him home and his dick in his pants. She understands what he needs. Same for a woman who feels insecure; a man loves her for that fact and makes her secure and finds the root of the problem and loves her thru it all.

BLACK WOMAN

Do you see how the shift has come into play? Back in the day, the media pushed the image of the European woman as a thing of beauty. Fortunate for me, I grew up in a household that taught us to love us. I am the only one of my siblings who took on my father's father's skin color; everyone else is darkskin and I hated being my color. I wanted to be like my brother and sister. My mom was a beautiful queen and she is my beautiful version of perfect, just like you, with every curve and deep rich color. It's a trend for so many, now trying to worship and be like, you are, sunkissed and loved in history all over the world. And it's not a fad, but they want us all to think so. Now they have to bear witness to the Original Woman, the Queen, Mother and Creator of the Universe. From your essence we all come forth. So special. I plead with you to put away the foolishness, ratchetness and defaming behavior. They say an addict can only become clean when they 'want to,' so want better for yourself and you will have better. Know that you are the role model that these little girls see and want to be and also the poster child for the ugly that you portray when you have your ass all out for the whole world to see. Which one will it be? Prim and proper you say that's just not you. Well understand this, your talk and way you dress teaches a man how to treat you and that's the truth.

WIND BLOW MY WAY

When the wind blows, I pray that it comes in my direction, but first passes by you, where you stand or at an intersection close by. My evening would be complete; just a subtle scent of your perfume would do the trick, praying that the gale winds come sweeping by, volumetric and thick, to bring the essences of you right to my nose…lovely lilac, cinnamon with a touch of white rose, diamond, pear crisp, opium, heaven… Ah just to take it all in with one breath, rolling down my lung cavity; just picture me, in a trance daydream; at best, love the aroma that fills my chest as my mind races, seeing you in reality. I have visions of touching your beautiful face… winds I pray for you to blow my way.

HAD ENOUGH

We have had enough of gossip, hating and belly-aching of no good men and women. We have had enough of the rudeness and childish behavior. Men have become boys again, and women have become chatty little girls. Giving up all the goods they got thinking that they will land a man, and are mad when they receive boys disguised as men. We have had enough of the rhetoric, the words and prayers, but action is needed more than just words. We are tired of all of these things, just so tired. We have lost the ability to be stand up women and guys, trying instead to deceive and manipulate each other for our own gain. Remember, the time we knew real women and men? We have had enough of this shit but not enough love. You will be sent your helper, your friend and better half; holding out for this will cause the ones around you to laugh, and make light of your patience. Love is a marathon, not a quick run or race. Love speaks to your heart and not your face.

HOLD ON

Hold on and never let go. Nowadays we have so little good of others, so we hold on and make it count when you do give your heart, mind, attention, and self away. Keep the things you cherish the most real, real close. Remember the difference of wants and needs, something like a love song. Hold on to something that will both fulfill and make your soul smile within. You'll find heaven again, if only he can be your lover and friend.

A BEAUTIFUL NIGHT

Looking into your eyes, running my hand over your shoulder, brushing your hair to your back, massaging your arms, turn away from me as I grasp your shoulders, moving up and down your neckline, back and sides, releasing the stress of the day, guiding you to your stomach as my hands manipulate your skin, warming, cupping, smoothing, and picking, full body coverage following your body's curves, touching, sensually arousing your nerves... calm down, baby, I got this; in due time will we find ourselves in pleasure, we have to get to know each other, as my eyes and hands study your body, we catch each other's breath as our hearts beat as one, slowly...Yes breathe, smile as your body is now under my command, visions of high waves, sunshine in the mornings over pure white sands. I've touched every inch of your body and yet complete, soft to hard strokes from head to feet, time had elapsed and I pay great attention to detail, undergarments stay exactly where they fell, passion and pleasure what a complete delight, a virtual, kiss and full climactic explosion between us....such a beautiful night.

QUEEN

No man can rise higher than his woman, Queen! Allow me...here you go, as I dust off your crown, adjust it for your majestic heirloom of which all of creation was spawned and created, a fortress of knowledge, wisdom and understanding, which humanity's survival abides. You, my Queen, are the blueprint for all that we see on this earth and in the heavens, to the deepest depth of the oceans. I bear witness that all that came after you are no more than imitations of you, one of the greatest gifts God gave the cosmos! Eternally defined as the One Infinite, all attributes and names of all things good and pure. Bowing in your presence, I remind you that all that glitters is not gold. Hold on to your crown your majesty...we shall do what we are told.

PUSH ON

Good Morning, Family! Even if you don't feel like it's that type of morning, push on. Even if you don't have the energy to roll out of bed, push on. Don't feel like talking to anyone because it's gonna take a miracle to do so, push on. Mad at the world and cursing God as you rise, push on...Just remember this, you have more folks that love you than hate you, and the haters actually love you. They just can't stand how much they do, so it comes out as jealousy envy and hate, push on. You have a God, children, family, friends, and plenty of fans that love you. Push on!

COMPLIMENT YOU

Good Morning, Family! Make sure that when people speak of you that you give them a good reason to compliment you. Let your personality and character speak for itself, be always respectful and kind.

IN SPITE OF

Good Morning, Family! You have to dance and sing, in spite of it all. The world can be falling down all around you, people forsake you, lie, steal, cheat, slander, and misuse you, still understand that it's your duty to yourself to choose to be happy.

CENTER YOURSELF

Good Morning, Family! "What you focus on, you lend your power to," so channel your power to productive and positive things. Fix your mind on love, happiness, success, cognitive skills, clarity, ease and convenience, friendship, life, companionship, loyalty, goals and long term accomplishments. Stay business minded!

WE DON'T GET WHAT WE WANT WE GET WHAT WE NEED

Good Morning, Family! Know that your prayers may not be answered exactly in the way you planned on them to turn out. You have to remember that; maybe you were not ready for that job, that relationship, that car, or money at that time. Things may not fall inline for a reason greater than your need at that particular moment. Take it all in stride and just know that it is all in divine order; a lesson that you needed to learn, discipline and patience that you needed to work on, forces you to just wait.

A BLESSING

Good Morning, Family! When we lose, sometimes we win, even when it seems there's no way to get to the end, end of making ends meet, and end of the week. Just to do it all over again. A blessing when we lose? How can that be? When all that I have and had was what I needed to be? Damn, I really don't have an answer to that but I do know something about God's math, subtracting and adding and multiplying. It has a method to it and when HE is at work, it can be a wild ride. HE can separate us from things that we see as good and others where HE sees are just not right. All this tearing down it must be the time to make room for something else to fill this void and take over this space? Yes that is true, it's all true. It's up to us to accept it and not collect it and smile, because God will work on us for a long while. True indeed it will feel like we are going thru hell, but that is part of the process which I myself know of very well. So let me let you in on a little secret: HE controls everything and everyone, doing HIS Will by design, even though it will make you lose your mind...trying to understand. He still loves you, you being you, a simple woman or man. No matter what's going on, stay encouraged and ride it on out. There is Joy in the morning!

HARD TIMES

Good Morning, Family! That time when I lived check to check and my deposit never made it into my account, you see I was rushing trying to get back to my side of town to pick up my kids. Deposited my money into my account via the ATM. I paid $340 a week for daycare and couldn't afford another late charge, hell I was just getting by, being late on some bills and letting others slide by. I needed them watched so that I could make it to work just to keep up. All my money was going to daycare and bills, the money was never deposited into the ATM, there was an error...shortly after I left, it spit the money back out. $730 dollars, half of that I was paying daycare with and the other was to feed my children. I would just have to figure out rent for that month later...much later. To my surprise after shopping getting a cart full of food, my card was declined and even after two times I went to the ATM. My heart sunk into the bottom of my stomach to see that my money never made it to my account. I was left dragging a hungry 2 year old and 6 year old kicking and screaming out of the store. I lost count of how many times we would come home to a cold house, no heat or electric, turned off for non-payment. Those days where we had no water, heat, or lights, definitely built character, bundled up in my bed fully clothed, with all of our covers together.

A FRIEND

Subtle sweet memories, I know you can hear me now...I know you can hear me now...life is never a dull moment; times of great stress and great triumph. We win and we lose; most times it's a big win and an even greater loss. Don't worry your mind too much about the future, because it has already been written, so the path you take to make it may not be of your own planning it was already written. We are given the choice to take the path that best suits our current condition... two paths in a yellow wood and I am much more thankful for the paths that were laid in front of me, a marker of greatness or the path that will be my demise. Choose wisely, my friend, but either way they will lead you to your destiny, demise, not in the sense that your life will be taken, but a lifestyle will definitely change and no longer exist, caught up in this whirlwind called life as we sit back and reminisce, reminisce...Love, ain't it a grand thing, can lead you to do all things, cry, hurt, adore, regret, hate and sing the praises of the one, woman bearing a child one daughter, one son, Subtle sweet memories, I know you can hear me now... keep up the good work. No shame in this game of life; you will win; in me you will always have a friend.

KEEP A LEVEL HEAD

Keep a level head...that's what you will have to say to yourself from time to time, Things may happen in life, folks may get you upset and it may seem that things are just not going your way. Keep a level head because cooler heads shall prevail. Yes we are human and we will react and say things when we get upset that will raise our blood pressure to the roof, but keep a level head, free of worry, free of anger. Cool down, take a breath and Whoosh! Anger makes you delusional and your sight and thought processes become blurred. Keep a level head and things will turn out just fine.

WHO WILL CATCH ME?

If I lose my footing in life; my knees buckle and my feet start to hurt; long days and nights; lower back pains and headaches from bright lights; who will catch me when I let my inside voice out? Yelling screaming and cussing motherfuckers out, catching myself or catching a case; catch me when I'm only defending my race and skin that I am in all this agony and pain done by man and cries of a wo-man. Catch me when I fall flat on my face trying to get back up, humble myself and win this race, I stay running because if I fall I don't want my legs to fail me as this world, my friends and society, who will catch me? I ask you again? Heartbroken I need a fixer-upper, a craftsman one who works wonders with his hands. God is that Potter and HE has created such a man to come to the weak and needy, to keep things together and make one whole. Loving you dearly and soothing your soul, fully qualified to do the job, arms of an angel and arms secure enough, stable and assured that catching me is not a chore. Who will catch me catching a queen worthy to be held in these arms?

CAGED BIRD IS FREE

Good Morning, Family! I know now why the caged bird sings. To sing is neither joy nor sadness. Which owns the tempo, rhythm, speed or melodic tones? It can be both. It sings to its heart's content. Conveying a message high pitched and sweet, telling a story that we all know something of, tragedy, loss of a loved one, striking out on love, rebirth, sunrises, hopes that tomorrow will be a better day, hearts full of laughter, no more heartache loathing or dismay. Sing me a song; please connect with every fiber of which I am, little caged bird. I may not be able to articulate the feelings, put them into words' proper form. It's hard to see the silver lining of my story in the midst of this storm...I weep, knowing that one day, caged bird, you will fly free; your door will open and your soul will flee, no more time for me to watch you, marveling at your structure and enjoying your pitches, tones and vocal delights. Your time has come and you are now free to spread your wings...I understand your body was tired; the last song you sang is pressed on my mind forever...Caged bird, your songs will be the melodies, the soundtrack of my life, this life that you left too soon. I'll make sure I remember the sweet words, as I transcend...a westerly wind blows past me and in the hollows of trees the crisp air claps, high pitched sounds echo into screams. All sounds are distorted noises, as I have thoughts of you. Please ease my troubled mind; I need to hear the sound of your voice again and again, a joyous tone to drown out the ones of

sorrow. I heard a mocking bird sing today and thought of you, thanks for the reminder. His song helped me to see the beauty of life is surely not over. I have more work to do and will do it sharing my light, representing your life. Here's my promise to you, I will sing songs of joy, I will try...I hear you singing now because you are free, right outside my window...God bless us all; heavy hearts be lightened, let tears fall and cleanse our souls, they shall forever live in us.

TAKE IT TO GOD

Good Morning, Family! The world around you could drive you a little crazy, have you questioning the love of God and pondering...Why? Go to God with it! Anything that you need, want and desire, HE will answer your prayers in one way or another. I say that because HE may make you work for what you want and not just drop it in your lap. Have a Great Weekend!

YOU'RE DOING A GOOD JOB

Good Morning, Family! "You're Doing a Great Job!" Words of encouragement, acknowledging what you do, day to day that is of great value to yourself and those you care about matters. Many times, what you do gets overlooked, scrutinized, and devalued. Well, I say Congrats on a job well done! What you do is more than Great it is Enough!

I FEEL YOUR PAIN

Good evening...I'm here for you and understand your pain...There is no immediate or permanent comfort for your loss; I know when I lost my best friend, my mom, I could not function. Life was just living and worrying about how she dealt with it, her spirit, the shock of the hour, is a most grievous thing! Losing your loved one's physical body, their spirit lives on...I often wonder, when I see mist in the night or early morning, could that be her? Feeling the warmth of the sun shinning on my left cheek, could that be her giving me a kiss, while she combs my hair as she used to do when I was a little child?.. Memories don't live like people do; we will always have them here in thought and in love; the sun seems just a little bit brighter and the cool wind blowing across your cheek is the hug and embrace. Feel them around you, even more still, as I feel my loved ones around me, also. I love you and am praying for you and your family.

SERVE AND PROTECT

Just spoke with a black officer and my first question was, "What do you think of the recent shootings?" His response was, "Man I ain't stuntin that man. I done shot somebody before...but that right there was overboard! Why would you shoot him? It ain't like you don't have his car and all his information, that's why I stay empolyed I can catch up to him later, hell he gonna get caught! I was arresting a dude and he ran from me but I ain't shoot him, Over a blunt?! Shit! That ain't worth it. I shot a man who tried to kill me; he was all hypered up and was really coming for me; he ain't die, but I made sure I slowed him down. Yeah, that shit between black and white been going on outside and inside the force, but that's how it is. Most niggas know what they up against, act up with me...yeah we done beat the breaks off of plenty of them, but ain't shit worth killing nobody. It's just on a case by case, you know, but homeboy was running away and for what? At the end of the day that was uncalled for; we are taught to defend ourselves, but how you gonna explain that one in South Carolina? He had his information, the dude was not gonna get away, yeah he could have run away but they would have caught up wit him later... Shooting somebody for no reason at all? Man he needs to go somewhere and bag groceries he is not cutout to do this work."

NOT MY BUSINESS

Good Morning, Family! I remember when it used to be the thing to do, "Mind your damn business." What they did, hell I don't want to know who what when where how or why. I'm minding my business so I'm good. That used to be the code, way back then but times have changed. Nowadays it would help someone, well at least not turning your back and not saying nothing. Say something! You see it, record it, and spread the word, because no longer will injustice fall by the wayside. Because you know what? What if it was you in that situation and somebody just minded their own business? Today it's the difference between life and death or at least a decent account of what actually happened. Yeah, I know even when we have the facts all on tape and on social media for all to see, they come back with a verdict of not guilty. Damn shame that it has to be this way and no longer is it back in the days where you stayed silent and not say a word. Today you are speaking up for those whose poor screams would never have been heard, or even taking into account that their business is yours. You would want the same in return.

LOOKING OVER MY SHOULDER?

I was asked, "Don't you worry about someone doing something bad to you? Don't you get tired of looking over your shoulder?"

Looking over my shoulder? For what? Let me break this down to you. I don't care about someone coming after me or even trying to take my life; its part of the life that I live and you can't have no conscience or heart, because if you do, you may wind up dead quicker than you want to. Naw, I ain't worried about the consequences. Hell it's already hard enough out here living; I'm sure being dead would be a lot easier. No one expects me to do anything good with my life anyway, so if it happens it happens and I won't waste time worrying about someone killing me. If I think about it and let it consume my mind, then I might as well be good as dead. I'm living my life, balls to the wall and balling out until I fall out; either way I'm going to make the life that I have the best that I can; no guts no glory. Why should I struggle? I want the same things that you have. Yes I heard it all before, "I took the time and worked hard for it." Yes I know, but my time out here in these streets is very short, so I have no time to waste so I want mine now and any way I can get it, I will. Yeah, it's a possibility, a very high probability that I could get killed anytime and any place but I'm not thinking about it at all the money and good times consumes my mind. My age expectancy, they said, was 24 years old and here I stand at 19, knowing that I have a shot, at least a five year run, so I have to make it

count before the reaper comes and its lights out. Maybe I will die of a drug overdose, mixed with too much alcohol, I loved getting sauced on the weekend, burnt out, falling out, waking up the next day too bent, can't function. I'm at a loss; must've taken too may blue pills mixed with the happy ones, or maybe I died of racial profiling, being in the wrong skin in my twin turbo, gold laced classic rims, t-tops off so I can feel the wind. The cop shoots me, never even taking a blink as I sink back in my seat, bleeding out and having visions of dark angels taking me to hell. Taking me to a place I know ohh so well. Living below the poverty line, all my friends stayed fresh and I barely had any clothes, hand-me-downs that I would have to rotate during the week. A lot of hungry nights, the arguing and fighting I saw in the home, my mother being beat by her boyfriend, never having a father at home. That nigga must've thought he was too good for me, now I am a product of my environment, kicking up dust terrorizing anyone who runs up against me. I have a love for guns... love the way the sound echoes in my ears, deafening all of the hurt and pain, going on robberies and late night trips again, feeding the hunger because it wants to eat, and my heart bleeds so I make others bleed. In this crazy world, going nowhere fast, never looking over my shoulder, I wanna see it when it comes at me and I wanna know the exact time the next breath will be my last. This can't be life, so I will embrace whatever comes my way, even if it's meant for me to die. At least I lived the way I wanted to live and it was never a lie, never a lie.

IM GLAD

He expressed his feelings, "Man I'm glad I don't have to go thru what you go thru." Yes, I am sure you are glad; just imagine a world like this, a world you cannot escape because of the color of your skin. I have to worry about being killed by someone who looks just like me, or a police officer. Hell life ain't easy. I pine over if today will be that unlucky day, getting shot in the head for looking, saying the wrong words or walking the wrong way. Damn! Can you even imagine the amount of stress, being pulled over by a cop, trying to keep my heart from jumping outta my chest? Yeah I know, but this ain't even about complying and being polite. "You fit the description. Why are you driving down this road this time of night?" Hell it can be daytime, for all they care. Being black, driving black, wanna switch places? I bet you wouldn't. Yes, can you even imagine being pulled over for nothing at all, just a hunch that you could be trafficking drugs or have a suspended license or some made up shit they throw around? Imagine being harassed and thrown on the ground, just pulled out of your car repeatedly, beaten and given a ticket. Yeah, I'm sure you are glad. "Then why don't you report them," you say. But I have tried too many times to count. I'm all tried out. I'm tired of this shit for real. Now you say that this sounds like rhetoric. Yeah? How about changing places, then you will encounter the racist faces and we are not just talking a black and white thing. I have been beaten and harassed by all colors, equal brutality opportunists. Just looking at my skin and saying to themselves, "It's a free for all," but I don't get the justice I deserve, while they lie about their job to protect and serve. The good cops you yell out. Yes, but we are not talking about them; so lets not generalize. Take the time to see the world thru my bruised eyes and wonder why I'm mad and my temper is at its boiling point. I raise my hands and scream, "Don't shoot," but they still aim and point their guns, even when I'm down, dying

from what they inflict. Try being me for a day, something you don't want to do, I'm sure of it. I have to deal with the threat of going at someone who looks just like me. We have the same skin color but we are not family; treated like an enemy. One wrong move and you might get killed. Some long-lasting hatred taught to us during slavery, which is quite real. "How does this even exist till this day?" you ask. I answer you, "Simple, being taught and treated like your are not worth nothing makes you turn on and hate what you are and anyone around you, the perfect result of divide and conquer." Mental slavery has had more lasting effects than physical slavery ever did. I am a father now so I have to think about my kids growing up in this world and I have to prepare them so that they will fight plenty of wars on so many fronts. Can you imagine a life like this, something that you will never want? Yes, be glad that this was not your life; how would you survive, now that you see what I go thru on a daily. It is a blessing indeed to be alive, because I survived a mental, social and physical death that was meant to catch up with me in my young age. I just pray that I can make it to the next day everyday. I wish for the day I look back and be glad that I didn't have to, but for now I do.

SPEAK YOUR MIND

Good Morning, Family! Never hold your tongue when your soul urges you to speak on it. Speak on it! Let there be no mistake that you mean what you say and say what you mean. Find freedom in having a voice and expressing it! Don't let anyone disrespect you! Speak out on injustices! Fight for what's right and stand firm on your beliefs! Speak your Mind!

AUTHOR JAMES R SIMMS

Author James R Simms lets his readers dive into his very complex mind, sharing with them his innermost thoughts, giving inspiration and sharing with them thought provoking narratives. "Morning Coffee" serves as a vessel for him to just let some of his thoughts out. Believe me, if he let them all out, he will have enough to fill a library. This is his third solo published project with many more to come. Who knows he just may be on to something.

www.ingramcontent.com/pod-product-compliance
Lightning Source LLC
Chambersburg PA
CBHW020615300426
44113CB00007B/654